# BEGINNER EMERGENCY SURVIVAL PREPAREDNESS

HOW TO PREPARE FOR EMERGENCY, JOB LOSS OR A TOTAL COLLAPSE. IN TEN EASY STEPS, FOR LESS MONEY THAN FIRE INSURANCE

## JEFF KIRKHAM

## JASON ROSS

1
___

# INTRODUCTION

In rough numbers, the United States has experienced a massively-threatening event once every fifty years since 1776. It's likely that each person will experience one or two of these events in their lifetime. Baby Boomers have experienced three such events (World War Two, the Cuban Missile Crisis and the Collapse of 2007/2008.)

Almost every region in the United States experiences at least one form of lethal natural disaster every year. Many of these are blamed on climate change and, if so, we can expect natural disasters to continue to increase in frequency. Polar vortexes, fires, floods, hurricanes, earthquakes, tsunamis and volcanos. It seems that nowhere is safe from catastrophe as we roll into the third hundred years as a country.

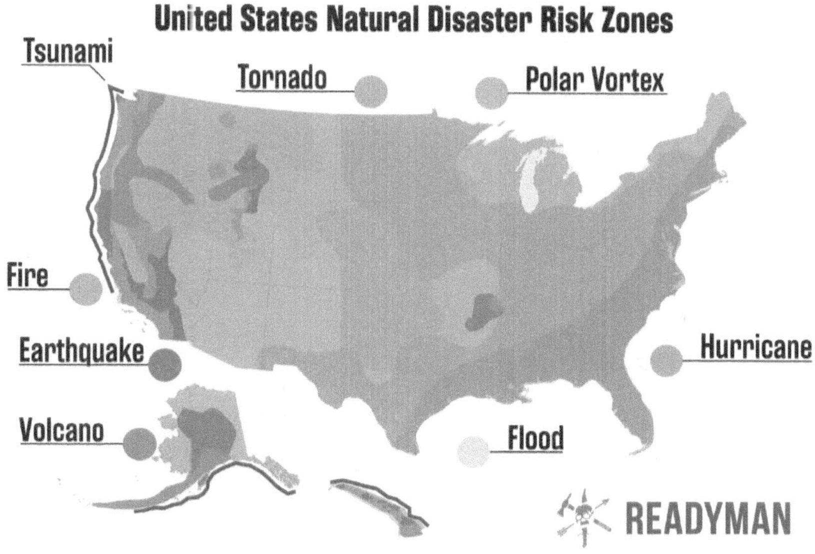


But even if you live in one of the dwindling emergency-free areas, economic disaster—during all our living memories—has crashed stock portfolios, evaporated 401K plans and devastated careers. There is no hiding from collapsing real estate markets and mounting debt.

Based on a combination of these factors, preparing for calamity can no longer be written off as being extreme, especially if done on a reasonable budget. Even the Department of Homeland Security urges Americans to prepare for disaster, and their warnings increase in seriousness every year.

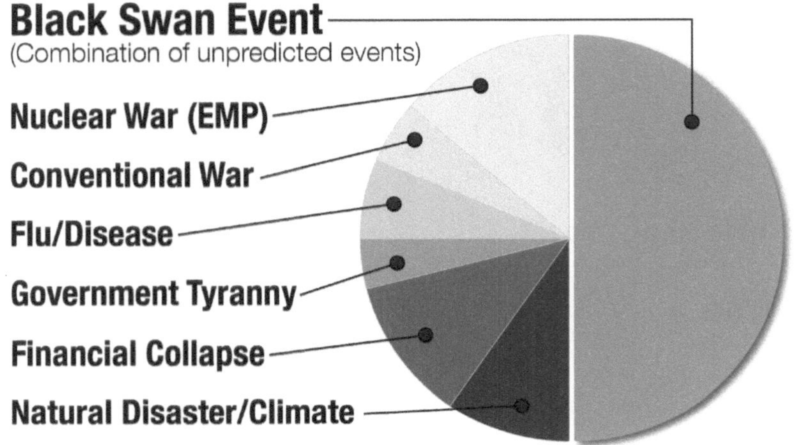



So, how much of an investment in your family's preparedness is reasonable?

American homeowners invest an average of $1,083 in fire insurance (homeowner's insurance) every year even though there is less than one-half of one percent chance of their house having any sort of fire in any given year (*NFPA report 2017). The chance of experiencing a catastrophic event that threatens the entire western economy *is four times higher* each year than your house catching fire.

We will outline a no-nonsense, step-by-step method to achieving basic security against any disaster—including a full collapse—over a period of six years while investing less than the cost of fire insurance on your home. In other words, less than $1,100 per year.

---

**Massively Threatening Events (USA):**

| | | |
|---|---|---|
| Revolutionary War | 1776 | Predictable War |
| Civil War | 1861 | Black Swan Event |
| World War I | 1914 | Black Swan Event |
| Great Depression | 1929 | Black Swan Event |
| World War II | 1939 | Predictable War |
| Cuban Missile Crisis | 1962 | Predictable Event |
| Collapse 2007/2008 | 2007 | Black Swan Event |

Seven events per 243 years (one event every 35 years) over half of which were Black Swan Events.

---

We recommend preparing a one year's supply of all basic needs, but the ten step process we outline builds layer-by-layer, gaining deeper preparedness for you and your family until you reach your one year's supply.

---

# Disaster Insurance
Insures against natural disaster, job loss, major collapse, minor collapse or Black Swan Event. Cost: only $1,100 per year for **Six Years.***

*Half of your premium is edible.

# STEP ONE: WATER

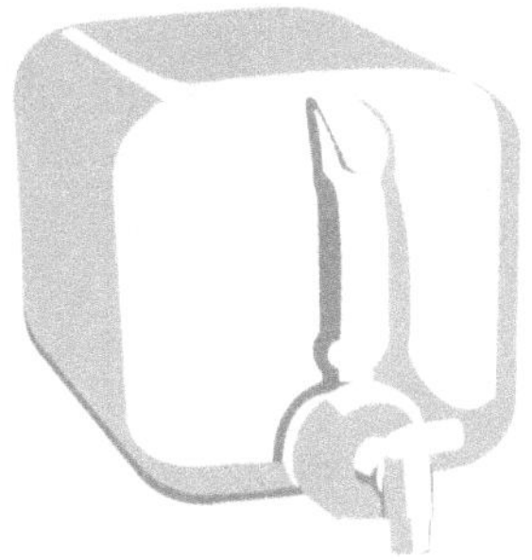

S TEP ONE: WATER STORAGE. Cost: $200*

EACH PERSON in a family requires a minimum of ONE GALLON of clean water per day, without fail. Doing bad math about water is one of the most devastating mistakes you can make, because it adds up very, very fast and going without water, even for a day, is crippling.

## Water Required:
### ONE GALLON per Family Member per Day.
### Minimum.

Bottled water gets consumed in the blink of an eye, but still, it's the first thing people grab off the store shelf in a disaster. Bottled water is not a good plan.

You can easily collect and hold about 50 gallons of water in your water heater and maybe 50 gallons in each bath tub, if you have time to fill them. Beyond that, you will need to invest in 55 gallon drums, which can be purchased from local classified ads normally around $20 each as repurposed food-grade HDPE2 barrels. Finding enough storage space around the home or apartment becomes the trick.

## Sample Math:

4 Family Members X 1 gallon/day X 365 days = 1,460 gallons (or 27 barrels*)

*Don't buy 27 barrels yet. There's an easier way.

**Rainwater**

Luckily, a LOT of water falls from the sky, no matter where you live—even in Arizona—so you will not need an entire year's supply of water in 55 gallon drums. Go to www.usclimatedata.com (or go to www.watercache.com and click on their rainwater catchment calculator) and click on your state to see your annual rainfall. Notice that rain does not fall consistently throughout the year and you will need to survive the dry times with water storage.

## Is your Roof Big Enough? (Yes!)

**Gallons per Inch of Rain per 1,000 sq. feet of roof:** 1,000 X 144 (sq. inches/sq. foot) X 1 inch / 231 inches per gallon = Gallons per inch of rain on 1,000 sq. foot of roof.

**Example:** Utah = about 1.5 inches per month except July & August. If we dedicate 2,000 sq. feet of roof:  2,000 X 144 X 1.5 / 231 = 1,870 gallons per month MINUS the amount we waste flushing out the gutters, etc.. Maybe we can count on 1,300 gallons per month, which is way more than we would need for a family of four (120 gallons.)

Collect rain water from the roof of your house and divert it from the downspouts into your empty barrels. You won't be able to collect ALL the water from your roof (because it's hard to get barrels to every downspout) but you should be able to collect enough to refill your empty barrels.

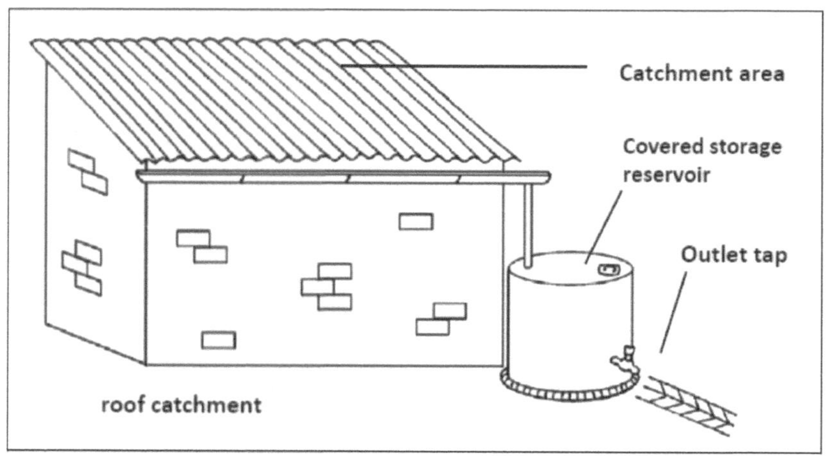


To divert water from your roof, you should buy and store

Collapsible 4-inch flex drain pipe ($23 for 25 feet) The drain pipe will allow you to cut and divert your rainwater downspouts to your barrels as you empty them. You can also buy in-line leaf guards that stop big chunks from falling into your barrels (search "rain harvesting" on Amazon.) Either way, the rainwater in your barrels should not be considered safe to drink without treatment.

**Treatment**

Water from your roof will have bacteria and your stored water will grow bacteria too. Nobody wants to get sick during a collapse. Anything you drink, you should treat, but that's easy as pie.

**Cheapest:** use bleach (8 drops per gallon, short shelf life) or pool shock (one teaspoon per gallon, long shelf life if stored right. $17 per pound). Generally, these are safe additives, but extended use might have negative side effects. Plus, the water will never taste particularly good. Buy pool shock at your local hardware store and stock up on extra if you want to be able to save your neighborhood from life-threatening diarrhea in a collapse.

**Cheap:** Ceramic stone filters ($9). Cut a hole in the bottom of a bucket, install the ceramic dome filter and it'll clean all but the toughest chemical impurities, which shouldn't be a problem unless you're trying to drink polluted ground water.

**Expensive:** Big Berkey Water Filter ($300) also filters many metal and chemical impurities.

## Boiling

You won't have enough fuel to boil water for long, so don't count on boiling. Plus, boiling water uses an incredible amount of heat energy. Using bleach or pool shock is easier and cheaper.

For less than $200, mostly invested in used, plastic barrels you eliminate the biggest shortfall in a natural disaster or a Black Swan Collapse: **water**. It's the cheapest, easiest preparation and there's no good reason not to do it.

# 3

## STEP TWO: CANNED FOOD

S TEP TWO. PACK YOUR PANTRY WITH CANS. Cost: $1900

FILL your pantry to the gills with a **three month supply** of the food you already like, and do it in canned foods.

The key to keeping the cost of a pantry down is to ROTATE the cans of food by eating them, then replacing them on your normal grocery run.

In general terms, the expiration date posted on most canned foods isn't true. Most foods will last at least *twice* their expiration dates. But you should eat and replace them long before they reach that date anyway, since you should rotate them.

To make rotating easier, purchase stackable rack organizers, eat the cans of food and then top the racks off.

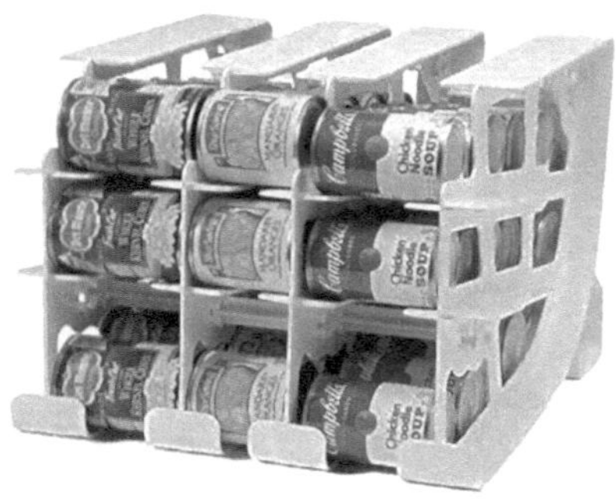

An even cheaper way to keep a supply of canned food is to learn how to bottle fruits and vegetables and even meats. Once you buy glass jars (Kerr Jars), a hot bath canning pot ($65, for fruits) and a pressure canner ($70 to $300, for vegetables and meats) your bottled foods become almost free, especially if you garden. If you love home-made jams and jellies and enjoy time in the kitchen, canning can be a lifelong hobby with incredible returns in fun and preparedness. Otherwise, begin by buying extra canned food from the store.

## 90-day Nutrition Requirement:
(for a 195 lb. Male)

**Needed Per Day:**

| | |
|---|---|
| Fats | 77 grams |
| Carbohydrates | 326 grams |
| Proteins | 71 grams |

**Needed for 90-days:**

| | |
|---|---|
| Fats | 6,930 grams |
| Carbohydrates | 29,340 grams |
| Proteins | 6,390 grams |

## 90-day Canned Food Checklist (190 lb. Male)

| No. Cans | Item | Fats | Carbs | Proteins | Calories | Cost |
|---|---|---|---|---|---|---|
| ☐ 10 cans | Clam Chowder | 200g | 320g | 120g | 3100 | $17.80 |
| ☐ 10 cans | Chicken Noodle | 50g | 200g | 75g | 1600 | $10.00 |
| ☐ 10 cans | Chicken Rice | 50g | 350g | 50g | 2200 | $10.00 |
| ☐ 20 cans | Beef Stew | 400g | 680g | 400g | 5000 | $48.80 |
| ☐ 20 cans | Chili/Beef | 400g | 1280g | 680g | 6800 | $26.00 |
| ☐ 30 cans | Refried Beans | 720g | 3240g | 1260g | 10500 | $46.00 |
| ☐ 15 cans | Roast Beef | 90g | 0g | 780g | 4800 | $41.10 |
| ☐ 15 cans | Chicken | 52g | 0g | 682g | 3150 | $48.75 |
| ☐ 30 cans | Tuna | 270g | 0g | 600g | 3600 | $35.7 |
| ☐ 10 cans | Corned Beef | 960g | 60g | 420g | 5800 | $27.00 |
| ☐ 20 cans | Peas | 0g | 1050g | 280g | 5200 | $20.00 |
| ☐ 20 cans | Green Beans | 0g | 210g | 70g | 1400 | $20.00 |
| ☐ 20 cans | Corn | 0g | 800g | 80g | 7000 | $20.00 |
| ☐ 10 cans | Carrots | 0g | 480g | 70g | 1000 | $20.00 |
| ☐ 10 cans | Potatoes | 0g | 740g | 100g | 1000 | $20.00 |
| ☐ 10 cans | Spinach | 0g | 280g | 220g | 1000 | $20.00 |
| ☐ 10 cans | Stewed Tomato | 0g | 700g | 70g | 1000 | $20.00 |
| ☐ 10 cans | Peaches | 0g | 600g | 0g | 2100 | $18.90 |
| ☐ 10 cans | Fruit Cocktail | 0g | 520g | 35g | 2100 | $18.90 |
| ☐ 10 cans | Pears | 0g | 600g | 0g | 2100 | $18.90 |
| ☐ 20 lbs. | Rice | 0g | 7000g | 600g | 32300 | $29.80 |
| ☐ 20 boxes | Spaghetti | 160g | 6560g | 1120g | 28000 | $20.00 |
| ☐ 5x40 oz. | Peanut Butter | 2625g | 1225g | 1225g | 33250 | $14.95 |
| ☐ 2x32 oz. | Almonds | 896g | 384g | 384g | 10300 | $16.98 |
| ☐ 1 bottle | Vegetable Oil | 672g | 0g | 0g | 8300 | $1.40 |
| Total | | 7,185g | 27,279g | 9,321g | 182,600 | $590.98 |
| ☐ Salt | | | | | 0 | $.89 |
| ☐ Pepper | | | | | 0 | $3.40 |
| ☐ Dried Onion | | | | | 0 | $1.69 |
| ☐ Dried Garlic | | | | | 0 | $1.69 |
| ☐ Hot Sauce | | | | | 0 | $1.00 |
| ☐ 5xKetchup | | | | | 7250 | $5.00 |
| ☐ Sugar 4 lbs | | | | | 7100 | $2.40 |
| ☐ 2x 12 oz. Honey | | | | | 2000 | $7.20 |
| Grand Total: | | | | | 198,950 | $619.25 |

**READYMAN**

# 4

## STEP THREE: DRY FOOD

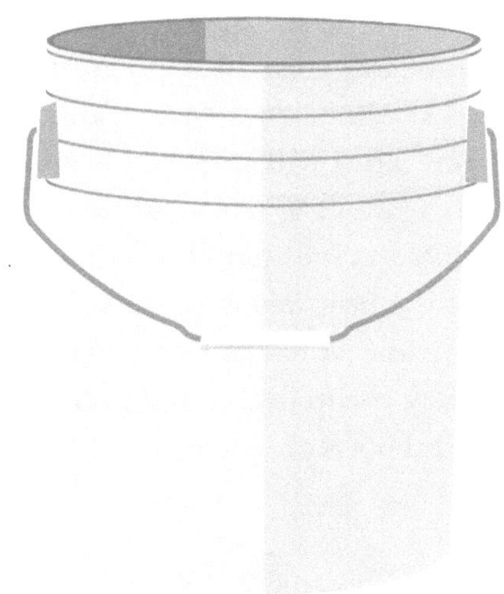

S TEP THREE. STACK YOUR BASEMENT WITH BUCKETS.
Cost: $350 per adult family member/ $175 per child (9 months
of food). Cost for family of four: $1,050

. . .

WITH THREE MONTHS OF "NORMAL FOOD" packed in your pantry, you need to fill out the remaining nine months with deep food storage. This is food you will probably never eat.

**Cheapest:** Dried food in plastic buckets—$650 per adult per year of food. Wheat, sugar, beans, corn, oats, potato flakes, veggies, fruit, dried milk, oils and yeast will all store for a really long time in plastic buckets without oxygen. They will keep you from starving, but that's about all. Remember: without a wheat grinder (and some way to power it with electricity) and without yeast, wheat isn't very versatile as a food. But wheat is the best way to preserve calories over time, as it probably lasts a lifetime when stored properly. And hard, red, winter wheat is very, very cheap (but rather difficult to turn into flour unless you have electrical power.)

**Cheap:** Mixed, pre-packaged food storage (freeze-dried plus simple dried in pre-packaged meals) from food storage companies—$2,000 (approx.) per adult per year of food. Soups, pastas, stews, casseroles, chilis, breakfasts... These are meals you may (possibly) rotate, since they're actually quite tasty and easy. They generally have a shorter shelf life then simple dried (20-25 years) since they have meats, proteins and processed foods like noodles.

**Expensive:** Primarily freeze-dried pre-packaged food storage (mostly freeze-dried in pre-packaged meals) from freeze-dry companies—$4,700 (approx.) per adult per year of food. Soups, pastas, eggs, casseroles, noodle dishes, breakfasts, etc.. The Cadillac of food storage, freeze-dried meals are high in sodium but generally delicious. Plus, they're very easy to prepare. Mountain House, the big dog in the freeze-dry industry, just bumped their shelf life to 30 years.

## Bulk Foods Shelf Life

| | |
|---|---|
| Wheat | 40 years, no problem |
| Dried Milk | 40 years, tasted great. |
| Honey | 40 years, no problem |
| Sugar | 40 years, no problem |
| Drink Mix | 40 years, same as sugar |
| Corn | 30 years |
| Pinto Beans | 30 years |
| Rolled Oats | 30 years |
| Potato Flakes | 30 years |
| Fruit | 30 years, but not very good |
| Flour | 30 years |
| White Rice | 20 years, starts to taste musty |
| Noodles | 20 years, nasty flavor |
| Peas | 20 years, tops |
| Olive Oil | 2 years |
| Peanut Butter | 2 years |
| Veggie Oil | 2 years, tops |
| Yeast | 1 year, toss and replace |

**Shelf Life**

Dried or freeze-dried food storage has at least a twenty year shelf life and most has a forty year shelf life, if stored in a cool, dry place. The actual shelf life varies based on the kind of food. We have tested twenty, thirty and forty-year old dried food storage and here's what we found:

Very few people rotate their deep, dried food storage because it's a pain in the butt to prepare and it's not what people normally eat. The cost of deep food storage should be amortized, for budgeting purposes, over about 30 years and then be re-purchased.

How to Buy

For the cheap, dry food storage, in small family quantities, it's easiest to buy the bulk food at Costco or someplace similar. If you're doing a large group, find bulk food from a local restaurant supplier, or buy from both Costco and the restaurant supplier. If you're prepping a huge group, buy your wheat and rice directly from a farmer or distributor. This part will require some research, since bulk food buying is different in every area. You should avoid shipping costs whenever possible.

**How to Bucket**

There is some disagreement about which storage method of dried food is best. If you buy food from a mixed-freeze-dried company or pure freeze-dried company, you shouldn't worry about proper storage. The company will ship the food ready-to-stack in your basement. When you buy bulk food, though, bug eggs are usually in your bulk food. The trick is to kill those eggs and to keep all new bugs out while eliminating oxygen. If you buy dried food in bulk and on-the-cheap, here's how to kill the bugs and store your bulk food for long life.

**Buckets**

Buy five or six gallon food-grade buckets from a local plastics supplier or buy them second-hand through the local classifieds (cheapest) when restaurants or bakeries finish using them. Clean the buckets and disinfect them before using. New, a five gallon bucket should cost around $4.11 plus the lid, and a six gallon bucket should cost around $4.73 plus the lid. Lids should cost around $1.70 new.

Eliminate Oxygen

For food to store long-term, you must remove the oxygen from the bucket once the food is inside. This also kills weevils and other bugs. There are two basic methods, depending on volume and your access to welding supplies:

**Flood with Nitrogen or Carbon Dioxide (huge scale, cheapest)**

Rent a bottle of nitrogen or $CO_2$ from the local welding supply and fashion a wand to flood the bucket with nitrogen after you fill the bucket with food. Then close the lid. This method requires no waiting.

Be very careful with Nitrogen or Carbon Dioxide that you do not use them in an enclosed area as they can result in unconsciousness or death due to suffocation.

**Flood with Dry Ice (medium scale, cheaper)**

Buy dry ice at your grocery store and break it with a hammer into chunks about 1/6th of a cup in size. Fill the bucket with food and leave 1/2 inch space on top. Place about 1/6th of a cup of dry ice on top. Leave the lid cracked so the dry ice will turn to gas, fill the bucket and overflow. After about an hour, seal the lid. Check two hours later and "burp" the lid and reseal if the lid is bulging.

Like bottled $CO_2$ or Nitrogen, be careful with dry ice that you do not use it or transport it in an enclosed area as the increase in $CO_2$ can result in unconsciousness or death due to suffocation.

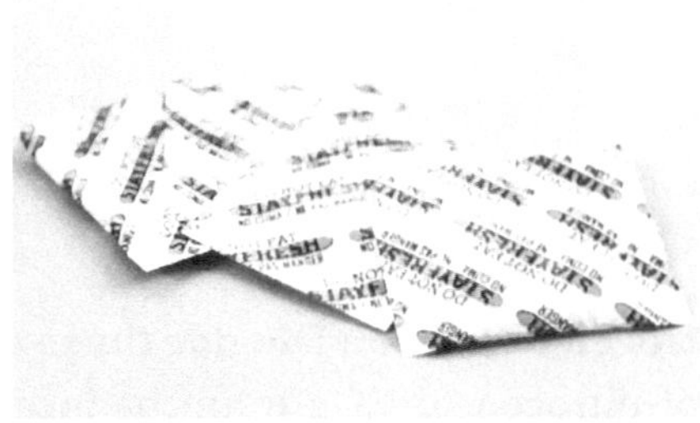

**Use Oxygen Absorbers (small scale, expensive)**
Buy oxygen absorbers (not desiccant) online and drop a 500cc oxygen absorber into each bucket. Seal immediately.

**Mylar Bags**

Some say that putting mylar bags inside the bucket help with preservation. Given the long, long storage times, there's really no way to know for sure. All our tests of 40 year-old food storage were simple #10 cans and plastic buckets without mylar bags. Our recommendation: if you're an anal person, use mylar bags. Otherwise, don't worry about it.

ONCE YOU HAVE ABOUT TWELVE, five gallon buckets per adult stored in your basement, filled with cheap, dry food, your "insurance policy" will have taken a giant leap forward.

By now, you should have invested $3,400 (for a family of four) and have three years into preparing. You will have your family's food and water set for a year of hard times, which might be all you need. The next seven steps will deal with other dangerous contingencies besides food and water, which may or may not turn out to be "optional."

> **Click to Download Nine Month
> Dry Food Storage Checklist
> or Download at:
> www.SubscribePage.com/Checklists**

> **Click to Download
> One Year Dry Food Storage Checklist
> or Download at:
> www.SubscribePage.com/Checklists**

# Dry Food Storage NINE MONTHS

| NINE MONTHS | Lbs./Adult | Price/Pound | Adult | Child |
|---|---|---|---|---|
| **Grains** | | | | |
| Wheat | 130 | $0.26 | $33.80 | $16.90 |
| Corn Meal | 19 | $1.46 | $27.74 | $13.87 |
| Quick Oats | 8 | $0.61 | $4.88 | $2.44 |
| Regular Oats | 11 | $0.61 | $6.71 | $3.36 |
| Rice | 38 | $0.52 | $19.76 | $9.88 |
| Spaghetti | 8 | $0.95 | $7.60 | $3.80 |
| Macaroni | 8 | $1.01 | $8.08 | $4.04 |
| | | | | |
| **Sugars** | | | | |
| Honey | 2.25 | $2.83 | $6.37 | $3.18 |
| Sugar | 30 | $0.60 | $18.00 | $9.00 |
| Maple Syrup | 1 | $3.59 | $3.59 | $1.80 |
| Corn Syrup | 2.25 | $0.61 | $1.37 | $0.69 |
| Carrots | 4 | $2.66 | $10.64 | $5.32 |
| Potato Flakes | 4 | $1.33 | $5.32 | $2.66 |
| Apple Slices | 4 | $4.84 | $19.36 | $9.68 |
| Onions | 2.25 | $2.52 | $5.67 | $2.84 |
| | | | | |
| **Fats and Oils** | | | | |
| Shortening | 3 | $1.50 | $4.50 | $2.25 |
| Vegatable Oil | 1.5 | $0.75 | $1.13 | $0.56 |
| Peanut Butter | 3 | $2.27 | $6.81 | $3.41 |
| | | | | |
| **Milk** | | | | |
| Dry Milk | 53 | $1.89 | $100.17 | $50.09 |
| | | | | |
| **Legumes** | | | | |
| Black Beans | 8 | $0.64 | $5.12 | $2.56 |
| White Beans | 8 | $0.64 | $5.12 | $2.56 |
| Pinto Beans | 8 | $0.74 | $5.92 | $2.96 |
| Dry Soup Mix | 4 | $7.33 | $29.32 | $14.66 |
| | | | | |
| **Cooking Essentials** | | | | |
| Baking Powder | 0.75 | $4.00 | $3.00 | $1.50 |
| Baking Soda | 0.75 | $0.78 | $0.59 | $0.29 |
| Yeast | 0.4 | $4.14 | $1.66 | $0.83 |
| Salt | 4 | $0.55 | $2.20 | $1.10 |
| Vinegar | 0.4 | $2.00 | $0.80 | $0.40 |
| | | | | |
| | | | $345.22 | $172.61 |

# 5

# STEP FOUR: DEFENSE

S TEP FOUR. PROTECT YOURSELF. Cost: $480

WHEN THE MODERN societies of Argentina and Venezuela collapsed, both experienced extreme civil disorder and violence. The same thing happened during the siege of Sarajevo. In these modern examples of collapse, protecting oneself and one's family became of paramount importance. The same could easily happen in the U.S. during a Black Swan Event. Remember: just because we haven't seen it before doesn't mean that it's unlikely. Depending on how you feel about that possibility, physical security could easily be a life-or-death priority.

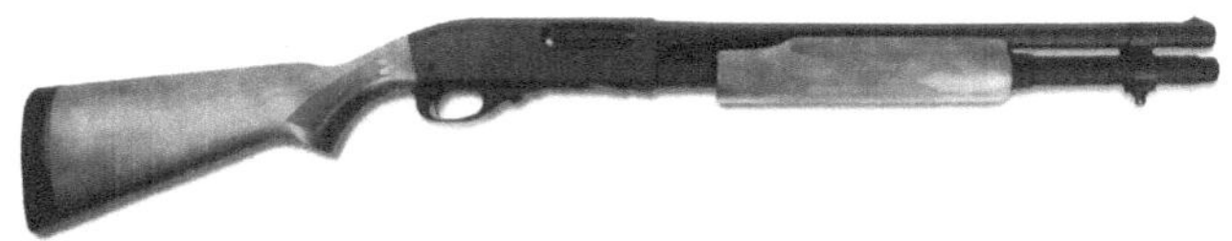

### Firearms

If you already have experience with firearms, then you likely have opinions and preferences. Stick with those and practice with what you know. If you aren't already well-versed in firearm use, then we suggest the following:

- **Get a shotgun to protect your home.** Handguns are good for concealment, but they're incredibly hard to use under stress and require at least twenty hours of training per year in order to employ with any real confidence (scared and in the dark.) Rifles are easier to use, but their bullets penetrate building materials to an extraordinary degree, making them very dangerous weapons in homes and neighborhoods. Shotguns are very easy to use (scared and in the dark) and light shot doesn't *usually* over-penetrate building materials.

- Shot shells filled with small shot are still quite lethal and do not usually over-penetrate building materials. We recommend the Remington 870 Express Tactical 7 Round shotgun ($443) and a box of Number Six shot shells ($8.) Any kind of firearm REQUIRES basic safety training or that firearm can become a liability to your family. Seek help at a local gun range before checking a firearm off your list. Somebody at the local gun range will be more-than-happy to teach you firearm safety.

- **Get bear spray or mace ($30).** You may be willing to train on a firearm, but what about family members who don't have that training or don't want it? Bear spray or mace are formidable weapons and are often the only weapon you need in case of an intruder. Even better, bear spray and mace are non-lethal. Blasting your teenage daughter's secret boyfriend in the face in the middle of the night can be cleaned up afterwards with a minimum of tragedy. Anyone can operate a can of bear spray, even without practice, which makes it the perfect weapon for those without firearm training and a great option when lethal force is not required.

## Community

Here's where preparing can get weird. One of the most potent weapons against civil disorder is a tight-knit community. Building a community that prepares for civil disorder means talking to other people about a Black Swan collapse. Talking about something so potentially terrible can feel macabre and strange.

Even so, the simple math on the risk of a collapse does not lie: the odds of a collapse are CERTAINLY not zero percent. They are *much higher* than zero percent and we would argue that the odds of a collapse hover around once every fifty years, or *two percent per year.*

Still, deep in human psychology, we have resistance to news that's negative and frightening, no matter how solid the data. Nobody wants to talk about a collapse at garden parties. If you do, you probably don't belong at garden parties.

At the same time, it's easy to talk about natural disasters—fires, floods, earthquakes, tsunamis and tornados. Every part of America experiences some sort of natural disaster risk and people are generally okay discussing preparations for natural disasters. Those disasters are on the news almost every day, so they're easier to accept.

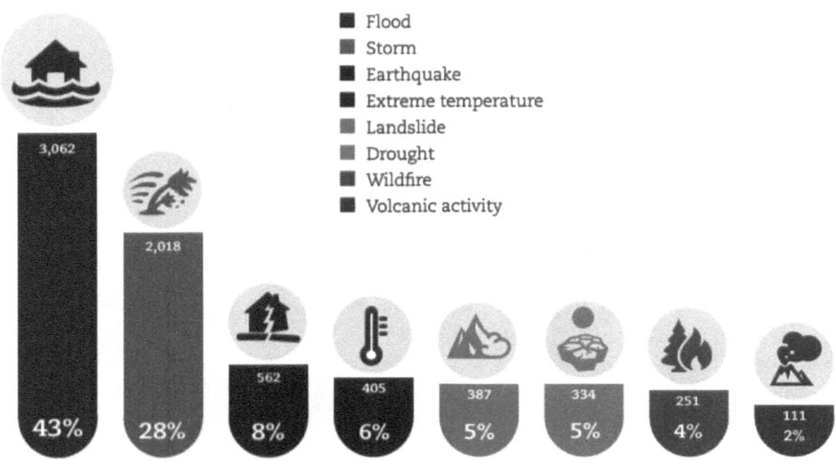


Organizing a response to a natural disaster comes very close to organizing a response to a Black Swan Event, and you can accomplish 80% of what needs to happen for a full collapse by preparing for a natural disaster. Your local neighborhood HOA or church group could be talked into preparing for natural disaster when they might've turned away from talking about a social collapse. When in doubt, don't push it. Someone in your community group (church, school, HOA, town) might already be organizing for a disaster. Get on board with their plan and it becomes even easier.

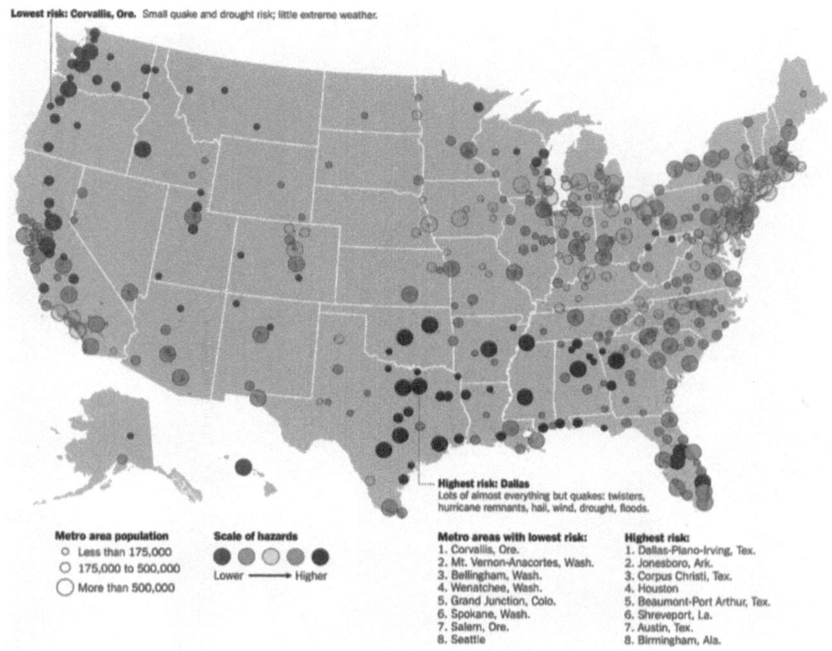


*Natural Disaster Risk, USA. New York Times

Organize your community around emergency preparedness and you will have added one of the greatest defenses available: good friends who don't panic during a crisis. In Argentina and Venezuela during their social collapses, the folks who did best weren't hiding out in the wilderness. Those people actually suffered worse than most. The people who did the best lived in friendly neighborhoods that looked out for one another. To protect your family, no gun in the world can compare to a trusted group of neighbors. Best of all, organizing your community to prepare is *FREE*.

# STEP FIVE: FOOD PREPARATION

## S TEP FIVE. GET COOKING. Cost: $250

WITHOUT GRID POWER, you're going to struggle to cook your food storage. Cooking over an open fire consumes far, far too much fuel, which you will cost thousands of calories to collect, chop and split. Here are two better options than an open campfire:

**Gas Camping Stove**

Coleman Dual Fuel Camping Stove ($117) uses either unleaded or Coleman fuel and sips gas, cooking many dozens of meals for a gallon of gas. Ultimately, you will run out of gas, but if you conserve gas for the purpose of cooking, the Coleman is an excellent option. If you cook on your Coleman about two hours a day, you will need to store 105 gallons (two 55 gallon drums) of unleaded fuel for an entire year of cooking. It's a tremendous amount of gasoline, and it must be rotated through your mowers, OHVs and cars so that it doesn't turn to varnish after a year. Storage of gasoline around your home may be illegal in your location, or frowned-upon. In any case, you will need to secure gasoline carefully to avoid an accidental fire, maybe using and locking metal barrels. Remember, you will also need a pump for your gas barrel, such as the Fill-Rite Rotary Hand Pump ($139).

We do not recommend propane cooking stoves, since the burn rate on propane is impractical for any long-term collapse, consuming a staggering amount of propane in just a month or two.

**Wood-burning Rocket-style Stoves**

If you have access to firewood, the rocket type stoves pull air across your burning wood creating a much more efficient heat than an open fire. There are many smaller rocket stoves, but the shepherd-style tent stove such as the Guide Gear Outdoor Wood Stove ($100) will conserve wood, heat your living space and cook your food all at the same time. Don't forget, you will also need a good chainsaw ($175), axe, sharpening puck, splitting maul and possibly a log-splitter if you're going to be burning firewood every day.

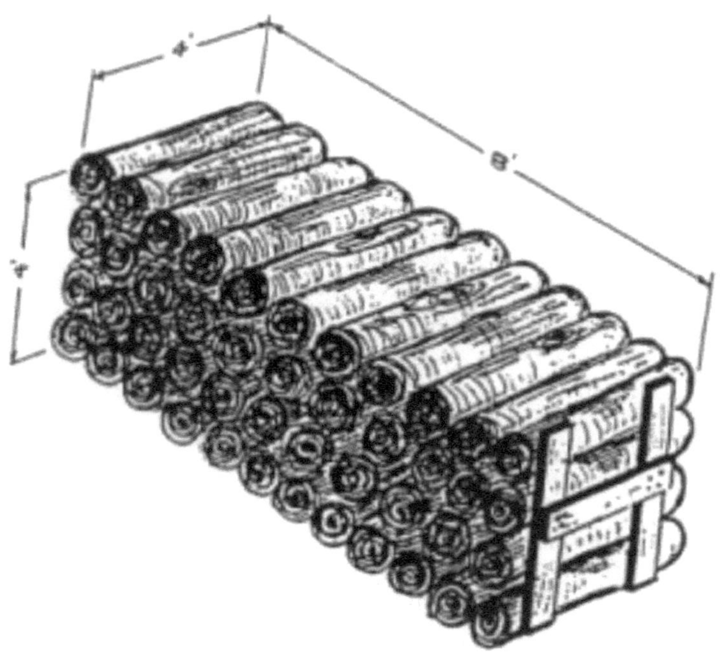

**One Cord (128 cubic ft.)**

For cooking, we recommend the Coleman for short-term emergencies, such as natural disasters, and a cylinder-style shepherd stove for long-term emergencies. This approach requires that you cut and store probably six cords of wood, but it reduces the need for gasoline, which is apt to go bad anyway.

With a wood-burning option on-hand, you can forego the 55 gallon drums of unleaded gas and use gas stored in normal 5 gallon gas cans instead since you'll only need 20 to 30 gallons.

# STEP SIX: PROTECTION FROM WEATHER

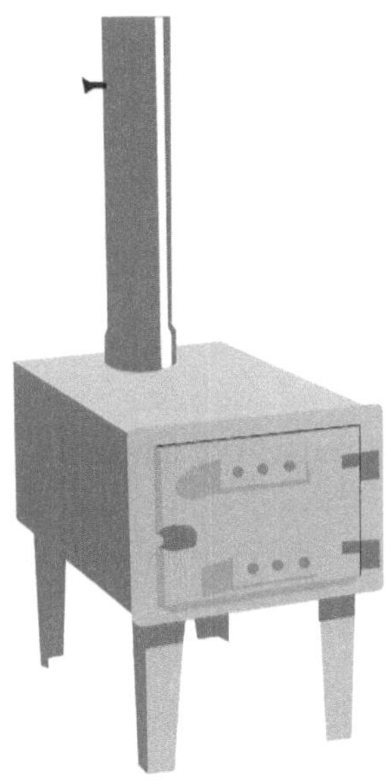

S TEP SIX. STAY WARM & DRY. Cost: $200

. . .

IF YOU'RE able to stay in your home during a disaster or collapse, it should keep you dry, which is a huge survival advantage. Being exposed to the elements deteriorates a family's odds of survival significantly.

There is a chance that you will be forced from your home by natural disaster, violence, or chemical/biological threats, but leaving your home and taking all your preparations with you would prove difficult or impossible—but we will address that contingency later.

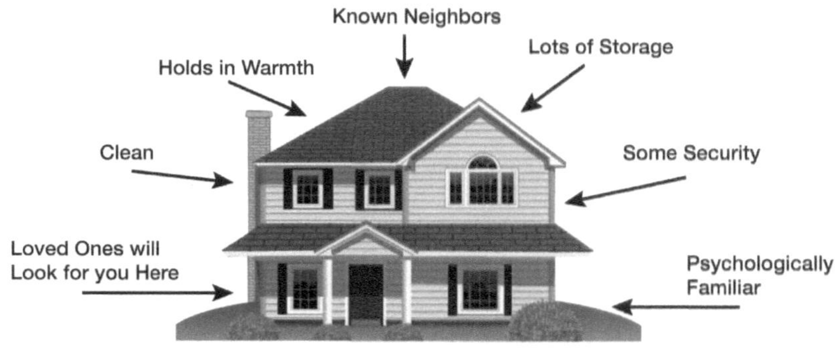


**Advantages of Staying Home in a Disaster**

For starters, your plan should be to stay in your home, since so many survival advantages have already been built into your house including dryness, cleanliness, storage space and comfort. Finding a dry place to treat wounds, warm up or rest while running around the countryside could become difficult and dangerous. So long as conditions permit, staying home is usually the best bet.

Depending on where you live, staying warm inside your home in the winter, spring and fall could be a major challenge. Fortunately, many of the same tools you'll use to stay warm and dry in your home will help keep you warm and dry if you're forced to leave.

**Warm & Dry Clothing**

As proven by the homeless in winter, the best way to stay warm is to layer your clothing. A big, puffy jacket is less flexible than several layers of clothing. A big jacket is either **on** (because you're cold) or **off** (because you got too hot.) Layered clothing can be adjusted to perfectly match temperature and exertion levels. Plus, you probably already have all the layers you need in your closet, so layering is also cheap.

However, cotton and denim fabrics are not ideal for outdoor use in the cold and wet. Both fabrics stay wet once they're wet and then provide very little insulation. You may wish to add several of the following fabrics and clothing options to your closet with outdoor, survival living in mind. We didn't add the cost of these into your preparation budget above, because you'll likely provide your family with outdoor clothing anyway.

**Gore-Tex Outer Jacket ($250).** Probably the most-expensive clothing item, Gore-Tex fabric is worth the price. While even the best Gore-Tex won't keep the rain out indefinitely, it will keep the rain out—and allow your perspiration to breathe—better than anything else. A good outer shell is key to clothing layering systems, cutting the wind and keeping moisture off your insulation layers. Anytime you're forced out-of-doors in the cold or wet, your Gore-Tex jacket will be your primary shelter. The more money you spend on Gore-Tex, generally, the better protection you will get. Invest as though your outer shell could be your home away from home.

**Fleece ($30).** Fleece repels water and moisture, maintains insulation and doesn't cost an arm and a leg. Almost any fleece will do, as generally all fleece tops provide excellent insulation.

**Beanie ($20).** Keeping your head warm provides a huge jump in comfort and survival. Buy acrylic, polyester or wool beanies for the family. Avoid cotton.

**Socks ($22).** Cotton socks are a disaster waiting to happen. Acrylic, polyester and wool blends provide much better durability and insulation. Invest in good outdoor socks such as Darn Tough ($20 a pair.)

**Thermal Underwear Bottoms ($35 bottom only).** Your regular outdoors-style pants should be okay so long as they're not denim or cotton, but your legs will eventually get cold. Fight the cold on your bottom half with a pair of polyester or wool blend thermal underwear bottoms. We don't suggest the tops unless you have extra money because there are so many other, cheaper, ways to insulate your torso. For your legs, thermal underwear bottoms provide warmth without sacrificing mobility.

**Boots ($120).** There are as many opinions about boots as there are opinions about knives, which is to say "limitless." The lighter your boot, the less likely you are to blister, all things being equal. Heavier boots will be sturdier, but will generally wear harder on your feet. Our preference is to "split the baby" and go with lighter, less-durable boots, and to stock multiple sets in your closet. Merrell offers a range of light boots in their Moab line ($120) that go from very light and less-durable to waterproof and more-durable. The Moab boot is not suitable for snow. Snowshoes, such as the North Face Chilkat ($110) provide a comfortable, athletic snow show with a heel lip for use with snowshoes.

**Staying Warm & Dry in your Home**

Assuming a failure of electricity or natural gas, your home will probably become very cold in a winter disaster or collapse. Our homes were not designed to stay warm without central heating, so they return to outdoor temperatures within a couple days without gas or electricity.

For starters, most of us will need to shrink the internal space of our homes to make it possible to reach a livable temperature, restricting our movement to one or two rooms. This can be accomplished with duct tape and plastic sheeting, which might also come in handy for medical emergencies requiring quarantine (see Step 8 below.) With better heating systems, the usable space of our home can expand.

From least to most sophisticated, here are the heating systems you should consider.

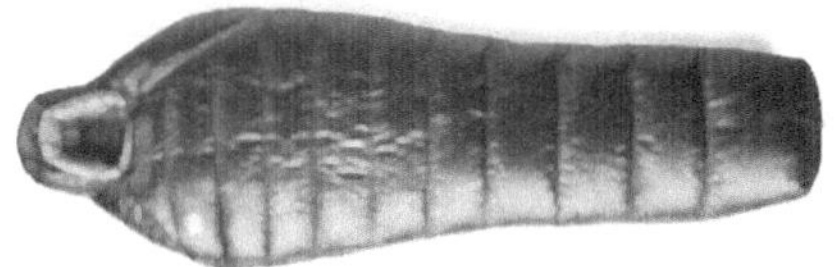

**Sleeping Bags ($40).** For sleeping in your home during a disaster or for sleeping on the run, sleeping bags offer a relatively cheap and portable way to insulate your body while your metabolism slows down during sleep. Pay special attention to the temperature rating on your bag and remember that a tent will add ten to fifteen degrees Fahrenheit to the bag's rating.

**Tent ($220).** Placing a tent inside your home, especially for sleeping, will capture body heat and provide an insulated bubble around your family. You may even wish to place a tent inside a tent inside your home to maximize the retention of body heat as a primary, cheap and easy heat source.

**Cylinder Stove ($200).** If you have a ready supply of firewood nearby, or if you've prepared a supply of firewood, you can heat portions of your home with a wood burning camp stove for a small investment. Modern household fireplaces, if you have them, don't offer much more than good looks. Don't count on modern box fireplaces to heat your home—they're usually inefficient and wasteful and they'll burn firewood faster than you can find it. A "Shepherd's Stove" or cylinder stove provides heat and a cooking surface. Plus, you can keep the cylinder stove broken down and stored in your garage. Don't forget, you'll need to plan to pipe the smoke out of your house, possibly through your chimney flue (try first.) Practice using your stove in the driveway, especially since most stoves require a break-in period to burn off the paint fumes.

# **ONE** Cord Of Firewood

**Firewood ($0).** You can usually find local sources of free firewood, but it'll require work. Without exception, people burn more firewood to achieve warmth and cooking than they imagine—burning six cords or more to keep one, small room warm over a winter in the snow. Six cords of wood is a stack of wood eight feet tall by eight feet long by TWELVE feet thick. That's wood for ONE winter for ONE room.

All your wood must be cut to length with a chainsaw and split for burning, which adds up to tens of thousands of calories worth of work. Do not count on harvesting wood from the inner city, because wood available in cities usually consists of green, live trees and hard-to-access construction material. Everyone would be hunting for dry wood inside cities, and competition would be fierce. Handle your firewood storage ahead of time and figure out a way to keep it secure if things go bad.

**Propane (not recommended).** While propane fuel can be used to cook and heat, the rate of consumption, if you do the math, is even scarier than wood or unleaded gas. Using propane to heat internal spaces is not practical for more than a few months unless you already have a massive propane tank and propane heating system.

# 8

# STEP SEVEN: ELECTRICITY

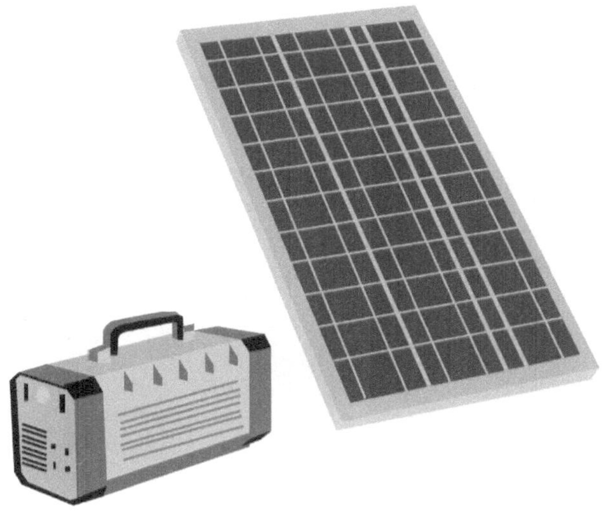

S TEP SEVEN. GAIN POWER. Cost: $380

POWER COULD BE one of the first things to fail in a Black Swan Event, and without power, you will lose the ability to see at night, communicate with family, read a map and run a power tool. Electrical power in a collapse can come from three, basic sources:

**Batteries**

Disposable batteries should be stored in bulk for all mission-critical devices such as flashlights, GPS, shortwave radios, two-way radios, weapon sights and aiming lasers. Rechargeable batteries work fine so long as you have also stored rechargers and solar panels to work with the rechargers. Test these systems in advance.

**Solar Generator**

To power small devices and to charge batteries, a solar generator like the Aeiusny Generator Portable Power UPS ($290) plus 100 Watt Solar Panels ($120), with a couple connectors, can provide survival-level electrical power. The next jump in solar power, to power appliances like a wheat grinder or refrigerator, is a serious jump and will require a working understanding of solar power. You can purchase an all-in-one unit like the Kodiak Solar Generator Kit ($3,000), but that might break your bank.

Building your own system can be done for much less, but will require that you understand how the appliance, panels, charge controller and battery bank work in tandem. The best way to design a solar system is to work backwards from the draws you plan to make on the system. In other words, decide what appliances you plan to power with your system, then design the system around that power need. The cheap way requires a little book learning, for which we recommend *Off Grid Solar*, by Joseph O'Connor ($15.)

### Gas Generator

A small, quiet Honda gas generator ($1,000) will provide reliable power sufficient to run a small grain mill until you run out of gasoline. Without a gasoline storage plan, the gas you have in the garage won't last long. Remember, unleaded gasoline goes bad in about a year—2 years with Sta-bil added, so gas must be rotated.

You may have noticed: food and power are connected. Wheat is your best food option when you consider price versus shelf-life and calories. However, hand-grinding wheat is not a great option. It's difficult and time-consuming even with a good hand mill. A powered grain mill like the Wondermill ($220) will make your life much easer, but there's a catch. The Wondermill requires 1250 Watts 120 VAC, which even the Kodiak Solar Generator Kit will barely satisfy, and will require a lot of solar panels to charge back up, depending on your sunlight.

Our recommendation is that you add up the appliances you hope to run (being reasonable) and contact a reputable solar provider such as www.backwoodssolar.com and ask the salesperson to help you design a system. For now, buy a small system like the Aeiusny for battery-powered tools and a hand grinder for your wheat (Deluxe Grain Mill, Victorio, $73).

# 9

## STEP EIGHT: FIRST AID

S TEP EIGHT. TREAT YOUR WOUNDS. Cost: $700

LUCKILY, the human body does a pretty good job of healing itself, especially if you keep wounds clean and dry. In modern society, we imagine every wound needs medical treatment, but humanity existed for eons without medical care and it worked relatively well since the body can handle most wounds and illnesses on its own.

With that said, there are some "easy fixes" provided by modern medicine that we would hate to do without. Most of these are cheap to stockpile.

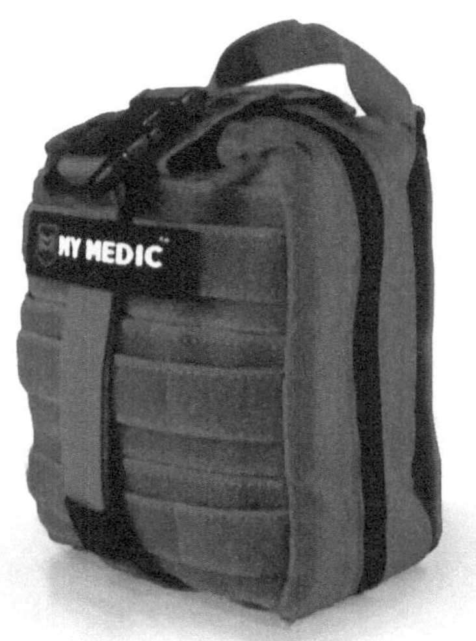

**Trauma First Aid Kit ($120).** To treat severe accidents and injuries, a trauma-oriented first aid kit can save the life of a loved one while you figure out a long-term fix. Gun shots, axe mistakes and power tool mishaps—all could lead to death if emergency responders are tied up or gone during a collapse. A trauma first aid kit such as the MyMedic MyFAK ($120) covers the major trauma needs (tourniquet, QuikClot, scapels, shock blankets) and is highly-portable. Also, the MyFAK contains "comfort" first aid such as band aids, creams, pain relievers and sting gels.

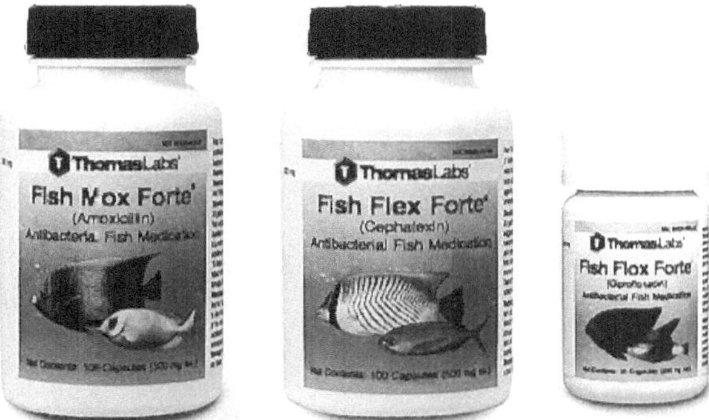


**Antibiotics ($210).** Once severe trauma has been addressed, there are few medicines as effective as antibiotics for helping the body cure itself. Even minor infections could take your life without antibiotics. Unfortunately, the American medical system does not trust adults to make their own decisions regarding the use of antibiotics, so antibiotics are a little hard to come by without a prescription. No matter. You can still buy antibiotics for your pet *fish* through an internet supplier like www.fishmoxfishflex.com and those antibiotics are functionally the same as human antibiotics. However, as a grown adult administering antibiotics to your family in a disaster, you must also know *which* antibiotics and at *what doses* to use them. For that, you must own and consult something like the books Antibiotic Essentials ($7) or Nursing Drug Handbook ($23). The Drug Handbooks are a good idea for anyone preparing for a collapse of the medical system. Antibiotics do lose effectiveness over time, especially in powder form. As a general rule, every two years you should replace your stored antibiotics.

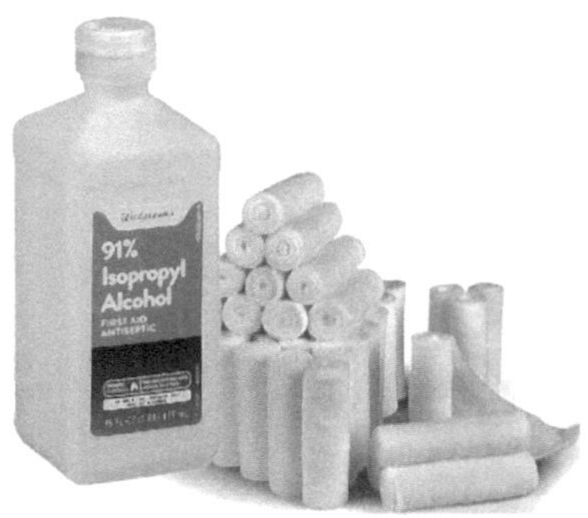

**Bulk Alcohol and Gauze ($150).** When asked what they would probably run out of first in a collapse, emergency room doctors usually respond: alcohol and gauze. Highly consumable in a traumatic emergency, isopropyl alcohol and gauze (in a variety of sizes) are consumed in quantity. Luckily, they're both pretty cheap to stock and easy to store.

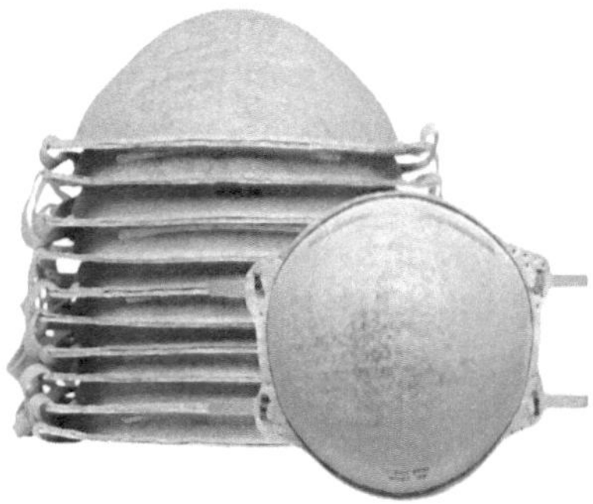

**Weird Medical Events ($120).** Preparing for a Black Swan Event means preparing for weird outcomes, especially when the preparations are cheap. N95 masks will help prevent transmission during a serious flu outbreak ($20/pack). Duct Tape ($10) and plastic sheeting ($30) can help your family quarantine sick family members during an outbreak or protect your house from radioactive particles. Potassium

Iodide ($30) tablets will reduce the uptake of radiation by the thyroid. Though gas masks are the icon of preparedness, we think the risk of chem/bio attack isn't enough to justify the cost of a gas mask. But if you disagree, the Israeli gas mask ($35) offers a cheap solution.

# 10

# STEP NINE: BUG OUT BAGS

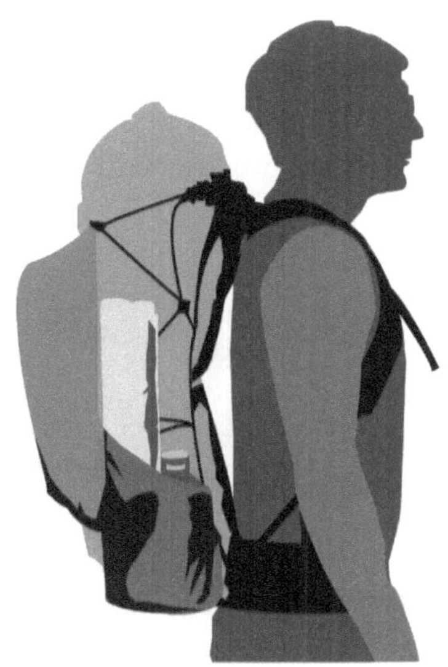

S TEP NINE. BE READY TO RUN. Cost: $1,100 approximately

. . .

With your basic preparations now in place, the next step is to prepare to leave it all behind. After all, we can neither predict nor control the outcome of a Black Swan Event and you must consider the possibility that your home may become unsafe, especially near a population center.

The million-dollar question would be: when to leave? If you leave too early, you could lose your preparations that aren't portable (such as firewood, a well or a large solar systems). If you leave too late, you could be marooned in a city with the roads blocked by traffic. The final preparation in our list is to provide your family the option to flee in a worst-case scenario.

**Bug Out Vehicle Totes: $900**

If you're forced to leave your home, the best option will be to flee in your vehicle. While most preparedness magazines champion hefty four-by-four trucks for bugging out, any car will do; especially a car with long range like a Prius or a minivan.

Most store a Vehicle Bug Out Tote in black, plastic totes in their garage where the totes can be thrown in the car at a moment's notice. You will still need to grab your Bug Out Backpack (below) and your

Grab Items (also below.) The Grab Items are things you will absolutely need— identification, guns and cash—but that aren't good to store in your garage.

*IMPORTANT NOTE: all the links below and in this book are *high value products*, meaning that we're recommending the best **middle-cost** product that we believe will do the job. If you sign up for the free ReadyMan Bug Out Bag Builder (Plan2BugOut), you will have the ability to customize your list with a higher or lower budget and see our higher or lower price recommendations for each product.

## BUG OUT VEHICLE TOTE CONTENTS:

- Heavy Rifle
- Rifle Ammunition
- Heavy Rifle Magazines (6)
- Heavy Rifle Sling
- Chest Rig (to carry magazines)
- Handgun (Open Carry)
- Handgun (Concealable)
- Handgun Ammunition
- Handgun Magazines (3 +1)
- Holster (Open Carry)
- Holster (Concealed)
- Handgun Magazine Pouch

- Tactical Flashlight
- Large Binoculars
- Water Jugs (full, at least 10 gallons/family member)
- Water Filter
- Water Additive (Iodine or Clorox)
- Lighters
- Backup Lighters
- First Aid Kit (trauma)
- Camp Stove
- Camp Stove Fuel
- Pot Grabber
- Folding Knife
- Fixed-blade Knife
- Knife Sharpening System
- Hatchet
- Axe Sharpening Puck
- Collapsible Saw
- Headlamps
- Multi-tool
- GPS
- Maps
- Watches
- Short Wave Radio
- FMRS Radios (2 or more)
- Extra Batteries for Everything
- Toilet Wipes/Toilet Paper
- Soap
- N95 Masks
- Gas Masks*
- Lip Balm
- Feminine Hygiene
- Caffeine Tablets
- MREs (Meals Ready to Eat)
- Mountain House Dehydrated Meals (4 days)

- Emergency Rations (2,000 calories/family member)
- Ground Coffee or Instant
- Creamer
- Spoons, Forks
- Plates
- Cups
- Paper Towels
- Sleeping Bags
- Sleeping Pads
- Gore-Tex Jackets
- Fleeces/Layer Tops
- Outdoor Pants
- Thermal Underwear (cold weather)
- Socks
- Beanies
- Boots (worn in)
- Leather Belt
- Sunglasses
- Work Gloves
- Warm Gloves (cold weather)
- Family Tent
- Camouflage Cover for Tent
- Spare Tire
- Tire Plug Kit
- Tire Repair Aerosol Cans
- Jump Starter
- Tool Set
- Fuel Siphon Kit
- Tow Strap

**GRAB ITEMS** (grab as you leave)

- Fill All Water Bottles
- Driver's Licenses, Social Security Cards and Passports
- Personal Medicine/Birth Control
- USB Cable for your Phone
- All Cash Possible
- Any Gold/Silver Coins
- Wear Outdoor Clothes, Boots, Leather Belt
- Sunglasses
- Guns and Ammunition
- Gasoline

# Which Bug Out Method to Use?
## Which Bug Out Method is Most Critical?

| Bug IN at Home | Bug OUT in Car | Bug OUT in Other Vehicle | Bug OUT on Foot |
| --- | --- | --- | --- |
| ⊕Keep ALL Preps | ⊕Keep Some Preps | ⊕Retain Few Preps | ⊕Almost NO Preps |
| ⊕Familiar Place | ⊕Fast Travel | ⊕Faster than Walk | ⊕Still Barely Mobile |
| ⊕Near Friends | ⊕Some Protection | ⊕Avoids Traffic | ⊖No Protection |
| ⊕No Travel Risk | ⊕Warm/Clean | ⊖No Protection | ⊖Wet/Dirty/Tired |
| ⊖Near Violence? | ⊖Traffic Jams? | ⊖Wet/Dirty | ⊖Very Slow |
| ⊖Target for Theft? | ⊖Enough Gas? | ⊖Enough Gas? | ⊖Target of Violence |

**Bug Out Backpack ($200)**

In the event that both your home and your vehicle become untenable, perhaps due to running our of gas or impassable traffic jams, your last-ditch option will be your Bug Out Backpack.

If at all possible, never abandon your wheels. A car provides not only transportation but shelter, a clean environment, a large cargo payload and some amount of ballistic cover from bullets. Living in the open may seem romantic, but it's exponentially more dangerous than being in your vehicle.

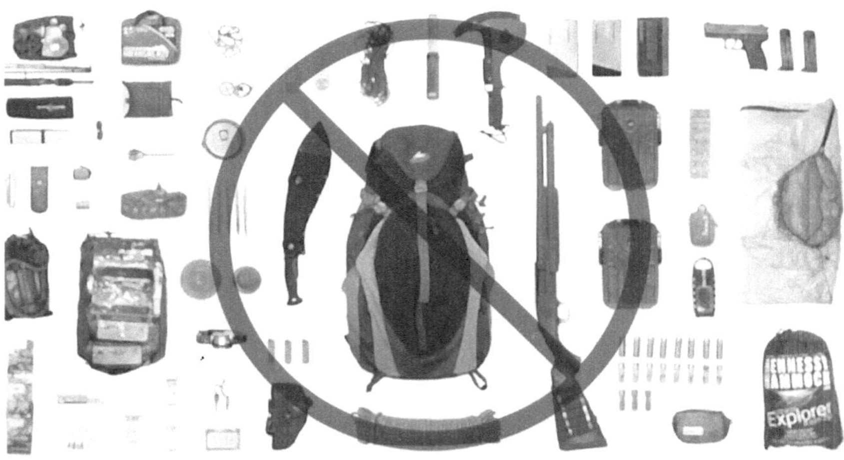

Bug Out Backpacks are not "wilderness survival kits." Surviving in the wilderness is nearly impossible, even as a single person in perfect weather. As a family, forget about surviving outdoors.

The only reason living in the wilderness *seems* like a good idea is because almost everyone spends their time indoors, so the wilderness seems empty during civilized times. Post-collapse, the wilderness would be full of people seeking any possible survival advantage, including preying upon other people. The wilderness is not where you want your family to make its last stand.

The purpose of the Bug Out Backpack is to get you and your family from where you get stuck to where you can survive long-term.

The fabled "Bug Out Bag" is exclusively for traveling from Point A (where it's dangerous) to Point B (where it's less-dangerous.) If you have nowhere to go, then your Bug Out Backpack will not be much help (see next chapter.)

Traveling overland, especially with family, is exceedingly difficult with weight on your back. Even for short stints, like backpacking adventures, feet, hips and backs are worn down quickly, leaving the traveller at the mercy of wherever his body fails. Cargo weight deteriorates survivability and range very, very quickly.

If you pack with more discipline, and avoid "cool" survival gear (such as beefy knives and romantic fire starters), you can get your backpack under **fifteen pounds** before water, food, fuel and weapons (here's how). The fifteen pound *base weight* threshold is critical for most adult males, as anything heavier generally grinds down the feet, hips and back at a surprising rate. No matter how strong or fit the adult, feet, hips and backs wear out. On the other hand, with a pack under fifteen pounds, a reasonably-fit adult can travel around thirteen miles per day with little body and joint stress. A fit adult can almost jog.

The quicker you reach your destination (sometimes known as a "Bug Out Location" or BOL), the more likely you will be to survive.

*AGAIN*: all the links below and in this book are *high value products*, meaning that we're recommending the best **middle-cost** product that we believe will do the job. If you sign up for the free ReadyMan Bug Out Bag Builder (Plan2BugOut), you will have the ability to customize your list with a higher or lower budget and see our higher or lower price recommendations for each product.

ULTRALIGHT BUG OUT **Backpack**

- Personal Medicine
- Lighters (2)
- Emergency Fire Starter Fuel
- Freeze-dried Food—Mountain House, 4 days
- Energy Snack
- Ultralight Water Bottles (2)
- Water Treatment Tablets
- Personal Water Filter (optional)
- Ultralight Sleeping Bag (proper temp)
- Ultralight Sleeping Pad

- Emergency Foil Blanket
- Cash
- Ultralight Alcohol Stove
- Alcohol
- Ultralight Tent
- Ultralight Tent Stakes
- Ultralight Pocket Knife
- N95 Masks
- Paracord
- Ultralight Toothbrush (cut down regular brush)
- Toothpaste (Tiny)
- DEET Repellent
- Toilet Paper/Wipes (Small)
- Extra Socks (1 Pair)
- Ultralight Pot
- Pot Grabber
- Ultralight Spork
- Ultralight Headlamp
- Backup Ultralight Headlamp
- Micro First Aid Kit
- Beanie
- Tourniquet
- Maps
- Compass
- Trash Bag (1)

**ReadyMan Plan2BugOut (Free)**

We would be remiss if we didn't emphasize the **FREE** ReadyMan Bug Out Bag Builder (Plan2BugOut) and tell you, quite humbly, that it's the best resource, at any cost, for preparing to bug out. It's a treasure trove of product and customization to your region and budget for building up all three levels of bugging out: in car, in an OHV and on-foot.

**Click for More Info
Plan2BugOut (free)
or Download at:
www.Plan2BugOut.com**

**ReadyMan Plan2Survive (Paid)**

Like the Bug Out Bag Builder, the Plan2Survive is a massive preparedness engine that helps you through each step of preparing to bug out and *actually survive* a long-term collapse or disaster. Part of the ReadyMan paid subscription, the Plan2Survive is ReadyMan's flagship offering, combining their massive body of survival experience from countless years overseas serving in Special Operations Forces (SOF) and an equal number of years preparing stateside. Among the over 1,200 skills, products and supplies described and linked in the Plan2Survive, ReadyMan members find a sensible and time-tested progression in seventeen categories of preparedness, all custom-tailored to your experience, budget, region, fitness level and community size. In a nutshell, it tells you on any given weekend what to buy, learn or practice **next** given your personal situation. Take the guesswork out of preparedness by signing up for the ReadyMan Plan2Survive.

**Alternative Vehicle**

Depending on terrain and weather, you may be able to prepare an alternative vehicle to your primary car—and that alternative vehicle could allow your family to stay mobile even with jammed up roads.

Bicycles, mopeds, motorcycles, OHVs (Off-highway Vehicles), snow machines or even a Radio Flyer wagon could serve as vehicles in case you lose your main transportation.

Again, an escape plan from your home is only as good as your planned destination. Leaving your home only to become a refugee is a very low-probability proposition, if past Black Swan Events are any indication.

# 11

## STEP TEN: BUG OUT LOCATION

S TEP TEN. FIND A HOME AWAY FROM HOME ("BOL")
Cost: $0

IF YOU LIVE in a large city, you might think your first order of business would be to flee the city in a collapse, and you might be right. However, if you've built up a trusting community of neighbors and friends who are prepared for a disaster, you should think long and hard before abandoning that huge survival advantage.

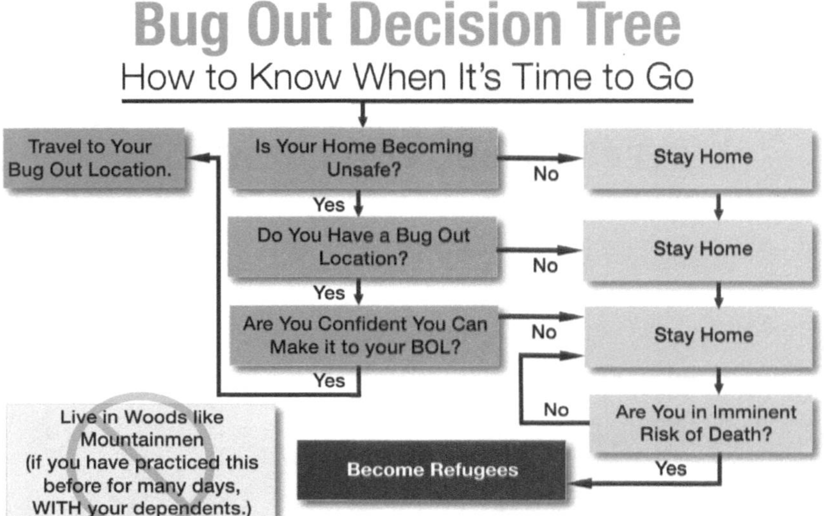


But no one can ignore the possibility of having to abandon their home. Natural disasters, nuclear attacks or civil disorder could render any location too dangerous. Eventually, everyone needs to plan for a "Bug Out Location" ("BOL.")

A small, rural town stands the best chance of being safe during a Black Swan Event. Small, agricultural towns (under 10,000 people) would likely maintain civil order and provide basic needs even in the worst collapse scenarios.

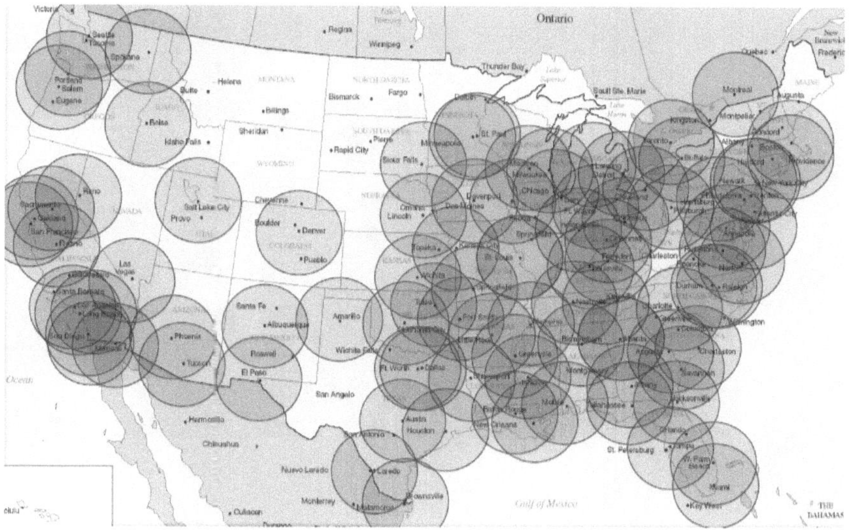

300 Mile Radius around each city greater than 100,000 population
(approximate range, tank of gas.)

The farther a small town sits from a city, the less pressure it might face from civil disorder, particularly if it's more than a tank of gas from a major city—around 300 miles. Very few small towns east of the Mississippi meet that distance requirement from a major city, but some small towns have other advantages, such as being easily defensible because of mountains, lakes, bridges or roads.

A neighborhood of cabins can also be a defensible BOL, especially if your family pre-stages your food and water storage at that location and has a solid "bug out plan" to get there.

It's not always necessary to *buy* a rural Bug Out Location. If you have high-value survival skills, such as a military combat experience, medical skills, veterinary skills, solar power skills, mechanical skills or even excellent square-foot gardening skills, you can often negotiate your family's place on a farm or a ranch property. Most farmers and ranchers are well-aware that our society could collapse and many are willing to discuss "what if" type of trade deals. If you have family or friends in a rural town, or if you *make new friends* in a rural town, you can work out an understanding where you provide supplies, equipment or skills that will benefit the farm family in exchange for taking you in if things go really bad.

Investing time and energy in a small town community and farm can bring rich dividends to your family—replacing beach vacations with rural learning vacations, where your family comes together while doing hands-on work.

Or, you could form a group time share retreat with a number of your neighbors, family or friends, where you all chip in on a rural property or cabin. The group could work together to have a fun vacation location that might also serve as a back up plan in case of job loss or serious collapse.

The options are endless and economical if your family is willing to invest in a community endeavor with family and friends. Truth is: we probably don't do enough of that kind of cooperating in America today—working together toward mutual benefit as friends or as a family clan. Figuring out a community relationship away from home could be the coolest thing you ever do for your family.

This step in preparation, unlike the others, can't be bought at Costco or Cabelas. Developing a home away from home can be accomplished without spending a dime, but it might require an attitude shift away from the individualistic, self-contained urban culture (which might be the most uncomfortable investment of all.)

At the end of your steady accumulation of supplies and skills described in this book, you might find you and your family gardening more, consuming less. Planning more, reacting less. sharing more, isolating yourself less.

Taking personal responsibility for your family's well-being and safety humbles a family in all the right ways—connecting them to reality and to earth. What starts out as a fear of a Black Swan collapse often transforms into a lifelong passion for the simple things: preparing food, taking care of health, keeping warm and befriending Mother Nature.

Maybe our American families need more of these simple things, after all. Maybe preparing for hard times yields benefits far beyond adding another insurance policy to the list.

(We can promise you: it absolutely does.)

# 12

# IMAGINE IT

We can only guess at what a collapse would really be like. Some few of us have experienced collapses in foreign nations, and some dwindling few experienced the American Great Depression. For a future collapse, we have only an inkling what it might be like.

One of the best ways to tease out the conditions of a collapse—be it mild or severe, economic or civil—is to read fiction. ReadyMan has an expanding collection of its own fiction works, the Black Autumn series, and there are a number of other post-apocalyptic, preparedness fiction books and series that present valuable perspectives on how-it-could-go-down. Here's a list of our favorites:

**ReadyMan Thriller Fiction:**

BLACK AUTUMN
BLACK AUTUMN TRAVELERS
THE LAST AIR FORCE ONE

**ReadyMan Recommended Fiction:**

SHTF Series, L.L. Akers,
(Cyber Attack preparedness)

ONE SECOND AFTER, William Forstchen,
(EMP preparedness)

DAY AFTER NEVER Series, Russell Blake,
(Criminal world)

GOING HOME Series, A. American,
(Bugging Out)

STILL SURVIVING Series, Boyd Craven,
(Rural South, Solar flare)

PATRIOTS Series, James Wesley Rawles, (Instructional fiction,
Government tyranny)

**13**

---

## GET EXCLUSIVE READYMAN STUFF

Our favorite part of this whole thing is becoming brothers and friends with our readers and members.

Our dirty secret: we don't write these books alone. We collaborate with scores of experts and fans and get many of our best ideas from readers.

Join Jason Ross' newsletter for information on new books and deals and a parade of insightful blog articles that shed light on everything from combat, to bugout bags, to how to get the most from a pastor at the end of the world. We might also throw in a ReadyMan gear deal or two.

Join our email list here. When you join, we'll keep you updated on new free stuff as well as stuff you can buy on Amazon.

In our biased opinion, ReadyMan has the most-informative, most-entertaining closed group on all of Facebook. If you read and enjoyed ***How to Survive a Black Swan***, you are *our* kind of person and we invite you to join the group by clicking the link: ReadyMan Closed Facebook Group.